# more than bread

*marya layth*

# More than Bread

An Illustrated Tale of
Poetry and Prose

Written and Illustrated
by Marya Layth

*More than Bread* copyright © 2017 by Marya Layth
All rights reserved. No part of this book may be
used or reproduced in any matter whatsoever
without written permission except in the case
of reprints in the context of reviews.

Inner Verse Press

ISBN: 978-0-9991808-0-8

Library of Congress Control Number: 2017911342

All artwork by Marya Layth
www.maryalayth.com

If, of thy mortal goods, thou art bereft,
And from thy slender store,
two loaves alone to thee are left,
Sell one, and with the dole,
Buy hyacinths to feed thy soul.


—Saadi Shirazi

To my family, for guiding me to the path less trodden.

To Rob, for traveling it with me.

# I

the tale 11
the poems 17

# II

the tale 51
the poems 57

# III

the tale 91
the poems 97

# IV

the tale 127
the poems 131

Vox Stellabrum

*an introduction*

The voices of the stars speak of many things, but never once have the stars spoken of the wishes wished upon them. No, not even the most ancient of secrets have left their lips. And perhaps that is why some stars explode. Perhaps it is that they can contain only so many of Humanity's mad desires before they themselves go mad.

But even if this were so, Humankind would continue to cast their secret desires—for such is a wish—to the stars. And the stars will continue to keep them. But all stars eventually die. And when they do, each desire wished upon them is finally released.

As for me, I find myself here—sitting.

Sitting beneath the stars—listening.

Listening for the explosion...
Listening for the revealing of secrets...
Listening for the voices of the stars
and for the depraved and the purest
of Humanity's desires harbored
within them.

# I

There once was a girl in pursuit of the perfect wish.

Eve after eve, The Girl sat beneath the night sky searching the City of Stars. Among its celestial citizens, she searched for a particular star to provide her with the particular information she needed for her particular wish.

Now you, dear reader, might think that it would make a great deal more sense were she to seek a fellow human for such advice. Surely, one's own kind could offer better insight.

Well, The Girl had thought of

this, and she had concluded that even if one did in fact know the perfect wish, one would not be at all inclined to reveal it—especially if one happened to be a member of the human race. And thus, The Girl did not seek human guidance but preferred to put her trust in the sky.

One night, while The Girl was scouring the astral metropolis above, a certain star gazed back at her. The Girl was more intrigued than she was caught off guard—and so, she kept its glance.

And just like that, the two began to converse.

"Strange girl, I see you here night after night silently looking at the stars but never calling upon a single one. I have decided to ask upon behalf of us all: Why?"

It seemed as though the entire race of stars resounded through the intonations of the self-appointed ambassador. As if all that were old and new were present in The Star's single voice. As if antiquity itself escorted the sound waves to her ears.

The Girl searched herself for the courage to respond to the celestial concord with her own solitary and utterly human voice. A voice she was just realizing was rather plain compared to the boundless manner of her acquaintance.

"Well, you see, I am silent because I am searching. Searching for a particular star. When I find it, I will wish my wish."

She hoped her response satisfied The Star's curiosity so that she could once again be left to her silence and to her searching.

It did not.

"Silly girl, perhaps you did not know; any one of us is able to grant you a wish. Now," The Star presumed, "tell me what yours is."

"Oh, but I couldn't possibly tell you my wish! I myself do not know what it is. I have no doubt, however, that when I find the star I am looking for, I will know."

"And precisely which type of star might that be?" The Star retorted, though The Girl was unaware of having said anything that warranted retorting.

"I would tell you but I fear it is rather...morbid."

The Star wasn't slightly but simply *was* offended—and also amused. That The Girl, a mere mortal, considered The Star to be not only inadequate to grant her wish but also too sensitive to handle a topic as frequent as death was both preposterous and enthralling to the mind of our celestial friend.

"I have witnessed more deaths than breaths you will ever breathe! Yet *you* fear for *my* sense of propriety? How curious..."

The undertones of vexation in The Star's voice finally became evident to her. The Girl thought she was behaving sensitively by not being forthwith when in fact The Star only felt belittled by The Girl's apparent need to withhold the truth. And so, The Girl resolved to speak candidly.

"No, please, it's just...I wait under the night sky for death. Not of my kind but of yours."

"Well, then, might I ask why you would wait for such a thing?" The Star asked, increasingly fascinated and perplexed—a state of mind The Star rather enjoyed.

The Girl paused.

She had never articulated aloud what it was that locked her eyes to the night sky.

*wander words*

A sage I am not.

I can only speak
of the aches I have suffered
to write this.

Of the heights I have flown
and have fallen from
to find these words.

Of the whispered ways
I have sought
in the meadow air,

and of the pandemonium
that vies for my ear.

A sage I am not.

I am only a witness
to whispers and noise.

## *found*

Dreamers.

All of us.

It's just that some of us
live the dreams they tell us
are the right ones to have.

The dreams that make us feel
*the same.*

The ones we secretly confess make us feel
*lost.*

Make us feel
*asleep.*

But what if we lost ourselves
to the dreams that make us feel...
*awake?*

The ones that make a difference.

Make *us* different.

And ensure we are anything but
*the same.*

I'm no gambler—

> the dice weighs
> too heavily
> in my hand.

But even I would wager
that we are meant to lose ourselves
to the dreams that make us feel
*found.*

## *traveler*

Before death escorts me home,
I will navigate through every paradox.

The most precarious of all
is how preaching can mislead
as much as silence.

I pray my words do not mislead you.

But if they do, know it was not my intent.

I, too, am trying to cope
with the burden and blessing
of Feeling.

*contending verdicts*

I have been judged,
time and time again,
as one terribly naïve
to the terrors of this world—

>ignorant of its
>*harsh cold reality.*

Simply because I am found,
time and time again,
lost in reveries
of a kinder way.

Well, perhaps it is *because* I see
just how tainted this world can be
that I cling so desperately
to all that is benign.

*cups*

I want to drink The Sun
in a million different ways
and wonder about how The Moon
spends its days.

I want to touch everything
that is real
and feel everything
there is to feel.

To view every vista
without ever having to open my eyes
and see the truth
despite all the lies.

But mostly, I want to play.

I want to play in every imaginary land—

> where the ones who mock believers
> in the reality unseen
> are the ones deemed devoted
> to the make-believe.

Because we live in a world
where The Sun is both
our ally and our foe—

> bringing light
> but also heat.

And they say if we get
too close or too far
it could kill us.

Oh, is it not just like reality?

If we get
too close or too far
it could kill us.

## *abcdefg : gfedcba*

When we were young,
we were told everyone should share,
should be healed,
should be kind,
should be free.

But now,
as older children,
it is rather radical
to believe such things
are the birthrights of you and me.

And it is not the bullies who are radical
but the ones who believe
that the air in our lungs should be clean
and that not all the soil beneath our feet
should turn to concrete.

Oh well,
for now, you will find me in the grass,
thanking each blade for its color
and asking each leaf to teach me of honor—

> for they shall not be bribed
> to stop cleaning the air.

Such integrity is so rarely seen
among my own kind.

I suppose I am radical too,
because I am still convinced
that everyone should share,
should be healed,
should be kind,
should be free.

To be a part of Humanity's
so-called radical legacy.

## *enclaves*

They thought her kind
to be a pretty lot of fools.

They would rather live to self-preserve
than to die preserving life—

*"Save altruism for the saints!"*
they yelled, over the voice
of their conscience.

They mocked compassion
because they feared the sacrifice
it most certainly entailed.

She feared apathy
because she knew it came with a sacrifice
much greater than death.

*tenebrae*

It is not darkness
that keeps me up at night.

It is that I am afraid of my eyes
becoming so adjusted to shadows
that I forget just how much
I need the light.

*bona fide*

They asked me to prove
the point of my existence...

...I asked,

"Why is it not enough
to embrace the wonder it is
that we exist at all?"

*amalgam*

I am often humbled
by this human frailty
but also awed
by the strength held
within these glass walls of
flesh
and
bone.

*sound of salt*

There are songs in the sea.

One in each grain of salt.

Violent and stilling songs.

I want to hear each one *(I need to)*
I need to feel all the ways my body can move
to the sound of newly discovered truth.

Or what if The Ocean herself *is* the sound?
And her choir of waves belt the lyrics
of each song of salt?

If I could speak her language
I would tell her how she sings in a way
that conquers me soothed.

How when she speaks
in the rolling tongues of sea,
it changes me in ways
I did not know needed to be changed.

And I might be a fool,
but I still know that no matter
how much I love her
she would drown me with no remorse
should I get caught in the spell
of her restive current.

Or have I missed the point?

Am I just begging for meaning?

You cannot see it, but God knows
how scraped my knees are from begging,
from hands that are often just...hands.

Well, why does it have to mean anything at all?

Right now, The Ocean is beautiful,
and that is enough.

## *asylum*

I have chased after the tangible
like it was all that mattered.

When all along
I just needed to see
that despite what they insist
I am much more
than
mere
matter.

*insurgency*

What if we discover that who we are
or who we want to be
will not give us waves of wealth
or a drop of power?

Well, what if that is okay?

What if we cannot be okay otherwise?

## glass bones

My home is with the broken people.

The ones whose backs have bent like mine
from picking up their pieces
over and over again.

We have so much to discuss—

> like how each time the pieces shatter
> they do so in different shapes and sizes.

How after each shatter
we have learned a new way to break
and a new way to be put back together.

marya layth

Only we know about the ongoing pursuit
of making peace with the pieces—

> with each jagged edge and fragment.

How though the method differs each time,
for the pieces never fall in the exact same way,
the first step is always
loving yourself
just a little bit more
than the last time—

> regardless if you stumbled
> over your own feet
> or if a thrown stone
> broke your glass bones.

*rewired*

I am not looking for sobriety.

I am looking to be so addicted to mercy
that I forget the use of a gavel.

To be so addicted to giving
that I forget the difference between us.

To be so addicted to faith
that I forget the high of fear...

...and even if I do not find it,
at least I am looking.

*ode to strength*

Oh gentle way,
will we ever come to you?

*the impossible task*

The hour will come,
just as it has in days long exhaled,
when I will be asked the impossible task—

to        love        my        enemy

For there is nothing Man has proven
to be more of an impossibility than that.

Nothing more rarely seen
since Herodotus recorded the passages
of the mortal presence.

Nothing more divisive
or more binding
than the cliché I risk writing about.

f    o    r    g    i    v    e    n    e    s    s

Forgiveness has the power
we have sought in fission,
but we do not need to split an atom
to make things whole.

And it sounds so simple
that it could not possibly be true!

But would it not seem that the truest truths
are always too simple to be trusted
by our faith in complexity?

Between you and me,
I am tired of measuring my days by time;
I would rather measure them
by how love and my heart rhyme.

Because right now the two sound uncouth
when spoken in tandem.

And so, I will say it again,
the hour will come,
just as it has in days long exhaled,
when I will be asked the impossible task—

to            love            my            enemy

Will I be only a matter of seconds away,
or will I be standing on the opposite hour
with the masses who live for the minutes?

Because that one hour
is the bridge that takes us
beyond the clock.

## *steady, delicate ones*

Envy is a most hideous thing—

but oh, how I covet the flowers,
whose petals remain delicate and intact
even as they endure nature's
most violent tantrums.

*of the places i can feel*

I inquired to the heavens,

"Why can't I see you?"

The heavens replied,

"Because you are
too concerned
with seeing."

## *famished*

You will never hear logic laugh more loudly
than at the one who suggests
the adulterer is no less than the sage,
the altruist no less than the libertine.

Your ears will ring for days

*(My ears still ring.)*

Because as much as I scorn this truth,
as much as the demons in me writhe
at the thought of a love so unconditional
that even the tongues dirtied
by their gossip of me
will be cleaned
and the hand of my abuser
will be held by the hand of God...

Still I accept it.

I must.

For my own sanctity
depends on such mercy.

I need to know that I can be unburdened
from the weight of my beloved sin—

    yes, *my sin*,
    that most untrendy word,
    which I see makes the masses cringe
    more than the lewdest thought.

Because The World has waged war
with my innocence
since the day It knew I was coming.

No, I need this to be true.

The truth is, I have never been
in such dire need of anything.

And even if I were to starve,
I would still need this more
than my aching body
would be in need
of its daily bread.

*inner verse*

I read what words were written
beneath my skin.

I read them all,
from blood to bone.

Only the verses beneath my heart
remain unknown.

The words are foreign but prophetic,
I can tell by their weight,
and they have my heart beating
in syllables of tongues that pulsate.

And I have this feeling I cannot feign,
that it is written in a language I once spoke,
but it would be easier to tame
the paroxysms of rain
than to remember this dialect
demanding to be uncloaked.

Though there are those
who have unveiled the verses on their own.

Except they cannot tell me what theirs say,
because the words were not meant to be read
*but lived*
in the very same way that The Sun teaches Light
not with speech but its rays.

I do not know a great many things,
but I do know this, and this alone—

>when I live love
>with my blood and bone
>the verses read a little less strange.

>And sometimes I can even pronounce
>the words that go beyond
>my voice's range.

## *the still is*

There is a truth that reigns
regardless of our knowledge of it.

And it has won every battle fought against it,
without weapons of the tongue or hand.

Oh Love,
you would even heal the countless soldiers
who have died in the ruthless pursuit
of your destruction...

...if only they would let you.

If only they knew
they were fighting you
in the first place.

*miles*

I am a nomad who,
compared to most,
has traveled The World little.

I have been too preoccupied
with traveling the miles,
which never seem to end,
within this skin.

Roads that lead me
where these aging bones cannot.

## *boxless*

I tore every box they tried to put me in—

box after box
after box after
box after box

I could not fit into one.

Each time another would rip to shreds,
it was always I who was deemed inadequate...
not the box for being too small.

For so long, *so long*,
I wanted to fit into the box.

Any damn box.

I believed the consensus—

that freedom would be found in there.

Until I tailored myself to fit,
I would remain outside,
ever brushing up against the edges.

Inside they are safe from edges,
because inside a square
edges become cozy corners
to curl up in.

But after being out here
I have had some time to ponder,
and I saw that The World is a sphere...
not a square.

A world floating in edgeless space—

>   where if we allow ourselves to realize it,
>   makes us feel like a paucity at best.

But in a box, we are big.

How melancholy it must be
to feel so big and so invincible
that there is nothing left
to be amazed by.

I prefer to be unfittable—

b      o      x      l      e      s      s

>   Small
>   and in awe of it all.

# II

After a few moments of heavy silence, The Star insisted,

"Girl, tell me why it is that your wish so depends on the final moments of a star's life? You might just discover that though I live, I can help."

The Girl knew the only way to escape The Star's inquiry was to relinquish her unique search, something she was unwilling to do.

"Well, you see, only a dying star can help me find what I seek. And what I seek is nothing more and nothing less than the perfect wish."

"And what makes you think that the death of a star will bring you any closer to finding this 'perfect wish'?"

As much as The Girl did not enjoy being interrogated, she imagined how much better she would understand her fellow man—and how much better he would understand her—if conversations between humans flowed with the fluidity of inquiry. Most conversations felt like rivers stifled by a dam of statements. Too many wished to be heard, rather than to hear. To tell, rather than to ask.

Finally, she replied,

"Oh, but don't you see? How could I possibly wish the perfect wish unless I have learned every wish Humankind has ever wished for? We both know only a dying star can grant me that...even if it is unwilling to do so."

The Girl wondered what question The Star would ask her next, but instead The Star's demeanor noticeably changed. It was as though the more transparent The Girl became, the less probing and more illuminating The Star's light felt.

"Dear girl, Humanity has been sharing wishes with us since the beginning of breath itself, and I can tell you: you are right to wait for our death. There is not a single one of us willing to reveal the wishes entrusted to us. Not while we are still burning bright. But I can also tell you this: hearing them will only confuse you beyond clarity's reach."

Incredulously, The Girl insisted, "Oh, but you don't understand—I *need* to know!"

"You mean to tell me that you have no wishes of your own? That you need to hear the wishes of others?"

The Star was just as determined to have The Girl divulge every last drop of truth as The Girl was determined to unearth every desire of Humanity.

"Actually, quite the opposite."

The Girl knew The Star would not cease its cross-examination until her bottom line was revealed. And so, that is precisely what she did.

"Well, you see, I once had so many wishes that my heart ached from the weight of their presence. Most of my desires were not unlike the desires of those around me. I have seen those very desires granted, and I have seen how *still* they are discontent. Even those who are more satisfied than others, they are mostly proud and comfortable, but so rarely do they have...joy.

"I finally decided that wishes are more like a threat, holding the happiness of the wisher hostage until their wish is granted, their desires fulfilled, only to awaken other dormant desires.

"Nonetheless, I cannot imagine a

wishless life. And so, I've concluded that wishes aren't the issue at all. Rather, it is what people wish for that pose the problem...

"And that is precisely why I sit out here, night after night, awaiting the opportunity to hear all of Humanity's desires. Maybe then, after I've listened to each one, I will know the one wish that has yet to be wished for...and I will wish for that."

The Girl suddenly shivered, but she was not cold. She felt that she stood before The Star with a naked soul. Only vulnerability cloaked her as she laid bare her heart's innermost qualms.

The Star remained silent, admiring The Girl's armor of transparency, thinking how The Girl's reasoning was more sensible than what most of Humankind generally deemed as logic.

## *lengths for less*

The lengths we go just to feel alive—

        for too many of us,
        the gift of breath
        will
                just
                never
                be
                        enough.

*honeyed spoils*

Faces contort, twist, and morph
when asked to taste the type of love
that forgives thy enemy.

Enraged when told
that it is stronger to be wronged
than to wrong.

For there are certain truths
that taste bitter...
        but only to palates
        that have become accustomed
        to honeyed spoils.

## *textile tongue*

Why do we go to such great lengths
to array ourselves in fine garments,
yet decorate our tongues with cheap words?

I do not know.

But I have heard we will not be content
until we use our words to sew torn hearts,
and loosen our grip on our own fine adornment
when asked to give it to warm another.

## *paper worlds*

It seems to me
a grave absurdity
that flesh starves
and cities crumble
from a lack of paper.

That we would devote each breath
to a way of life that brings out
time's more burdensome qualities
and our more
devilish attributes.

That we have no choice,
it would seem,
but to devote our lives to a world
that would tear us away from the homes
we live to acquire,
though rarely live in.

And that we all too often
find ourselves in that noble paradox
of putting the needs of proprietors
before the needs of our children—

    and yet, *for* our children.

Aside from this,
I have little to say on the topic.

For much has already been said,
and with better tact,
by the myriads before me.

It is all just so simply unpoetic.

## *the irony of euphoria*

And they would call me an idealist
when they believe euphoria
is something that can be purchased.

*sewing with dust*

Because too many of us
would mend our torn dollar bills
before mending our torn souls.

## *exchangeable parts*

Hatred is not the problem.

It is that we keep on falling in love
with those things that oppose love.

The lot of us would rather die

for money
for glory
for pleasure

than to live to love one another.

*roar of the lamb*

The roar of the lion rings
through the ears of lambs,
mocking them for being too meek
*to hear it like it is.*

But lambs know that the lion loves
the sound of its roar too much to actually
*hear it how it is.*

If only the lion quieted its roar
for just a breath,
then, maybe, it would know
*how it is.*

## *the everlasting tantrum*

Oh, it is a tragic thing indeed
when our toys become people.

Our playground, The World.

Our tantrums, war—

our most favorite game
of all.

## *spellbound*

Beguiled
by a fix
that will never
fix us.

## *poise and play / poison play*

Children demand fairness
*(the children within us still do).*

What a sorrow it is they are rarely told
that though The World is often unjust,
it is no reason to conform to its injustices.

No tear is held back,
and no opportunity to laugh
is lost upon them—

        all before The World will tell them
        that emotion expressed is unpoised.

Well, I would rather be unpoised
than to be riddled with the sophistication
of the decorous—

>who have forgotten that
>play
>and
>laughter
>and
>wonder
>and
>the array of simplicities
>we are all so unfamiliar with
>are the only riches
>worth accruing.

We had them once
*(and we could have them again)*,
when our hands were small enough
to hold onto all that is truly grand.

*the dividing factor*

Darling, don't you know
it is not death that divides us?

Death is the one force
that will humble all souls—

>    the prideful,
>    the greedy,
>    the reverent,
>    the kind.

It is how we live
in discordance with one another
that separates us more
than our mortality ever could.

*doorless kingdoms*

Heaven is not an external place
we are refused access to.

Heaven is an internal place
we refuse to access.

*a taste forgotten*

Let us not be so concerned
with selling the fruits of our beliefs
to unwilling palettes
that we forget the taste ourselves.

*a taste told*

But should we forget the sweet tastes
of the fruits we try to sell,
perhaps we are spending too much time
speaking of such fruits
and not enough time imbibing them.

*a taste tried*

And if it so happens
that our palettes no longer
enjoy the taste—

that is, if we speak of mercy,
yet prefer how resentment
lingers on our tongue...

if we speak of unconditional love,
yet perspire with contempt
toward the blessings of
the undeserving...

or if we speak of charity,
yet find greed making us tremble
with fear of how giving
will make us lack...

then let us, for the sake of honesty,
speak freely of our battles lost against Virtue.

For the one who can admit their shortcomings
helps the aspiring heart more than the one
who strives to appear righteous
but forgets to tell us of the strain.

*inevitable creed*

So many of us boast of how
we have no religion,
in that supercilious way that we do.

And yet, I know not one
who does not wish
the rest of the world thought
just
like
them.

## plight of the performer

The conceited heart is always yearning.

And even if the whole wide world were to clap
for such a soul at once,
it would complain that the applause
was not loud enough.

But the applause *is* loud...

Only, conceit *(that thief!)*
is louder than all of those clapping hands.

*the constant variable*

Is it not true of us all
that we split hairs till our fingers bleed
as we try to justify
why when we do $x$,
it is just,
but when another does $x$,
it is a most heinous crime?

*myopic vision*

We go about clenching magnifying glasses
until they are all but glued to our hands
and have impaired our vision
to the tragic extent
that all we see are marred versions
of one another...

        of ourselves.

           We shove each other beneath
              its distorting glare,
       magnifying one another's every move
to a degree our eyes are not naturally made
                  to see.

      For to focus only on one's blunders
is as foolhardy as focusing on one's single limb
      and claiming that it is the whole body.

So let us put away our magnifying glasses;
        for we know deep down,
     beneath all those layers of pride,
we would burn beneath the glare of another's.

*tactile*

Sometimes,
we are given
the golden opportunity
to embody the weaknesses
we deride in another.

Otherwise,
we may never learn
to embrace
compassion
over
judgment.

*expedience*

As if an eye for an eye
ever gave anyone anything
besides an orgasmic second
that thrills the body
only to leave it emptier
than the socket
from whom the eye
was ripped out.

*primal-portrait*

How frequently do we send words shooting
like arrows towards a loved one's back?

> We are no longer
> hunters and gatherers,
> but we are still the most skilled
> of archers.

How often do we find ourselves storm tossed
with that thunder-lust for flesh?

> The kind that makes
> even the most
> prey-like of us
> become predators.

And most of all, how rarely do we have
those sacred moments, the honest kind,
when we realize just how much
our preaching does not enlighten,
but blinds?

It is as though we cannot help ourselves
from judging those who refuse to conform
to our golden standards
that we ourselves struggle to attain—

    or are they just painted gold?

Do not assume I am speaking only of the pious
    *(for I know folks, both the God-fearing*
    *and the godless type, with equal zeal).*

No,
I myself have not reached such a state of virtue.

Have you?

But I will aim for it.
I will yearn for it.
I will write about it.
I will think about it,
until I do.

## armchair physicians

We ridicule The World
in the comfort of our homes,
much like I am doing now,
like doctors able to cure a disease
but are simply unwilling to do so.

*activism*

We cannot help but make a difference.

Even our indifference
makes a difference.

In fact, one might say,
it makes the biggest difference
of all.

## *labors of comfort*

It is not suffering
but the devotion to comfort
that is our greatest enemy.

For even birth, the miracle of all miracles,
is not possible without Woman's willingness
to endure the pangs of labor.

*cruel master*

There is a beauty that is sinister.
Fleshy. Enigmatic.
Unmerciful. Beckoning.
Rotting. New.
All at once.

And no matter how much
we sacrifice for it,
sacrifice *ourselves* for it,
it still seems to mock us.

*bread*

It is whatever or whomever
we sink our perfect teeth into.

It is whatever or whomever
we imbibe to fill the belly of our Want.

It is whatever or whomever
sustains us until our next feed.

Tell me,
what haven't our mouths devoured?

What poisons won't we sip to feel good?

To make the void go away,
if even for just a little bit.

Soil, blood, friend, or foe...
and if we could devour God
we would do that too.

Some believe we already have.

And so it goes that
we consume,
c o n s u m e
c  o  n  s  u  m  e
C   O   N   S   U   M   E

...are consumed.

Chewing our way through life,
making sure to leave a trail of crumbs
for our children to eat
so that they too can acquire a palette
for such seasoned tastes.

We will only applaud them
once they have mastered
the chase of crumbs, too.

All this consuming
because we don't just hunger...

we starve.

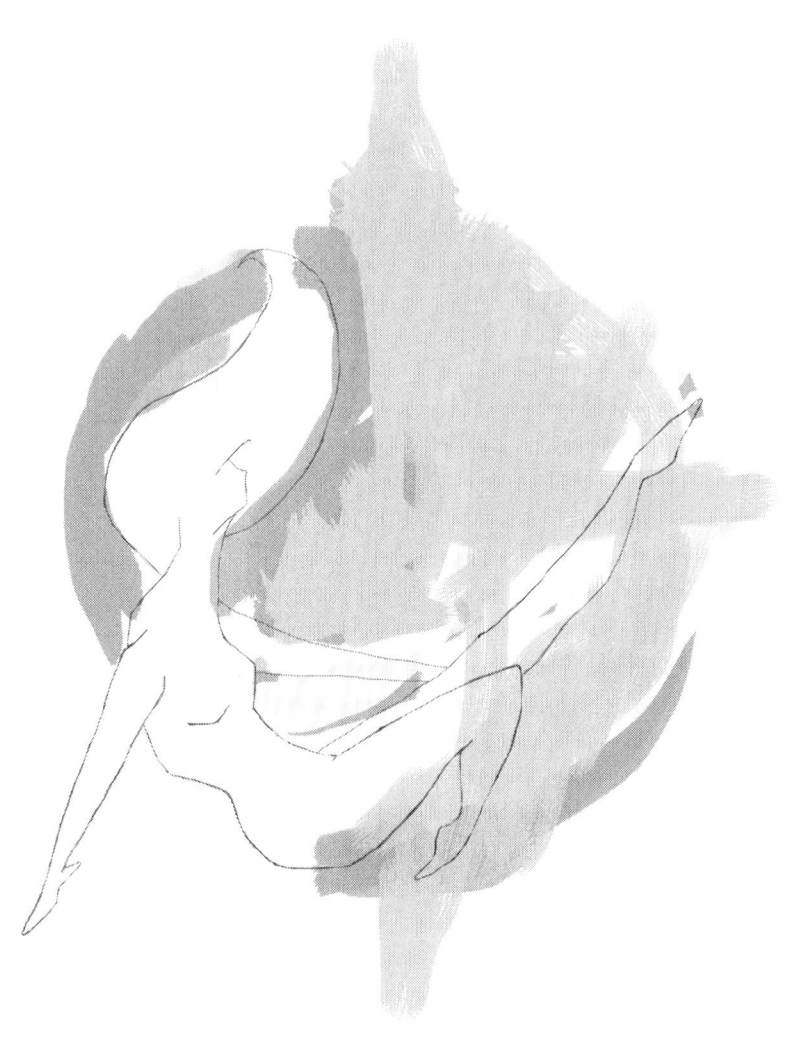

# III

The Star was fond of The Girl. She was equal parts principled, naïve, and convicted. She wasn't the type to start or even partake in a revolution, but The Girl was a soldier nonetheless.

There was an unusual bravery about her. A breed of courage greatly needed in The World. After all, The Star thought, there was a place in The Sky for every star, even the ones human eyes will never see. Why should it be any different on land? For The Girl was a type of soldier who observed others yet challenged only herself and, by doing so, took on all of Humankind.

But despite The Star's fondness for The Girl, The Star could not tell her what she wanted to hear.

"Oh sweet one, you would be better off if the entire sky were to come crashing down upon you than to know the weight of every heart. And even if, in this very instant, every star were to die and shower you with all of Humanity's wishes, I can assure you that you still would not be any closer to knowing what the perfect one is."

As expected, The Star perceived a shadow of dismay come over The Girl.

And so, The Star shed its light—

"Truly, the desires of your kind are no secret. They are all contained, if even dormant, within you. As for the freedom you seek in the perfect wish...well, you do not need a wish to achieve that."

"Then, please, tell me...what do I need?" The Girl supplicated.

Now it was The Girl who was determined to ask the questions.

"It seems you already know."

"I do?"

"You said it yourself: you must listen."

"But if not for Humanity's desires then for what am I listening?"

"I cannot hear it for you anymore than I can see or touch or feel for you. I can, however, tell you this: The World will tell you how to survive, if even comfortably and lavishly. This voice takes little to be heard. It is as ubiquitous as air, and what this voice teaches inspires the majority of wishes harbored within the night sky. But there is another voice, and you must *choose* to listen for it. This voice speaks of how to live."

"If not to survive then to live for what?" she asked, hoping The Star would clarify...

"For more than bread."

Confusion overwhelmed The Girl,
but she could tell The Star was not
going to explain much else to her.

Desperately, she uttered,
"What could that possibly mean?"

## *chrysalis senses*

Blindness is looking at a butterfly
and insisting it is still a caterpillar.

Deafness is listening to a confession
and hearing only sin.

Dumbness is speaking with eloquence
but not with love.

*bent to stand*

Stay inspired.

But mostly, stay humble...
humble in the presence of Everything.

So that even a grain of sand
ignites you with awe.

So that you can look
at your own hands with reverence,
because you realize how even the most
infinitesimal movement of a single finger
is just as complex as fusion
within The Sun.

So that,
keeping the vastness of The Universe in mind,
you can look at a blade of grass
and swoon at how it is rarer
than a shooting star.

*hum*

Hum to the sound
that inspires Silence
to sing.

## *preparing for combat*

Love is a weapon
too heavy to be held
by mortal hands.

It is a weapon wielded only by the heart,
used to combat not the hate in others
but that which is in ourselves.

*forward! quick march!*

Forward! Quick march!

Though they pursue you,
they cannot capture you.

You become their hostage
only when you revolve your life
around aiming at them.

Forward! Quick march!

Keep your gaze ahead.

Remember, you are not on the field
to win the battles around you.

You are on the field
to win the battles within you.

## *of the ebb*

Be sure of it:
the pain will pass.

But there is more pain to come.

Eventually, that pain will pass too.

And so on and so forth.

Even still, I will tell you
with all of the conviction in my bones:

it is okay...

it is *more* than okay.

*arise*

Do not cling to the ground
because you once fell.

Stand.

Stand tall.

After all, the best views

are

worth

falling

for.

## *demarcations*

By all means,
help them recover between fights.

Give them water.

Wipe the sweat from their brow.

Sew hope into their doubt-torn hearts.

And when you find it hard
to witness blow after blow,
ask yourself this:

How can a fighter know victory
if never given the opportunity
to face an opponent?

For there are legions within us
that carry a light so bright
it can illumine our darkest territories.

So, dear warrior, don't you see?

To remind them that triumph
is already within them
is of more help than if you were
to win their battle
and steal their victory.

*thread pillars*

Persevere, pure heart;
the sinews of the firmament
are sewn with the thread of your innocence.

## *grand tour*

If you scour the earth
for proof of your worth,
you should know it was yours
before your very own birth.

*certainties*

If only you knew...
that you were built
with Love,
for Love,
to Love.

*the intent*

Because you were not manufactured;
you were made.

## mantra of the lamb

No matter what people say,
no matter what they have
or have not done,
treat them well.

Treat them well for no reason at all.

In fact, it only counts as kindness
*because* you have no reason at all.

And what do *you* get out of this?

Wellness.

*incentives*

Before you cross that bridge,
you should know,
forgiving people does not change them;

it changes you.

## *unhindered day*

The end of day need not be mourned,
for your greatest joys will arise
when The Sun goes down
and you have learned to carry its light
into The Night.

## *trifles and tragedies*

Compassion is not a limited resource—

as if it were something to be saved
only for disasters.

Why not be compassionate for both
the trifles and the tragedies?

This way, trifles will not so easily
become tragedies.

## *withstand*

There will come a time
when someone criticizes
the beauty within you.

They will see your patience
and call you slow,
your kindness
and call you naïve,
your mercy
and call you weak.

Do not resent them for this;
they have yet to realize
the true meaning of strength.

marya layth

## *pews and pedestals*

Do not
mistake
the pew
for a
pedestal

for the
t w o
have as
much in
common
as the
o c e a n
d o e s
w i t h
l a n d

## word of honor

I cannot promise you
that there are no shadows;
neither God
nor Science
promise that.

I can, however, assure you
that should you position yourself
towards the light,
your shadow will remain
ever behind you.

Both God and Science,
promise that.

marya layth

*blueprints*

Whatever we do,
wherever we do it,
may we do it kindly.

## *beating walls*

If you are blaming Love
for those walls around your heart,
then dare I say, it was not Love
that did that to you.

Love never builds walls;
it only breaks them.

*mithridate*

You will understand
the most profound of wisdom
when you stop assuming
that it must be complex.

You will feel more loved
than you have ever felt
when you stop demanding
that it must be earned.

Darling soul,
stop.

So that you may
begin.

*heliotropism*

No matter how many times
The Earth turns its back,
there The Sun remains.

Steady and still,
despite this wayward world.

Though we are on The Earth,
let us live like The Sun.

marya layth

*eudaemonia*

Illness is to the body,
whose ideal state is health,
what cruelty is to the soul,
whose ideal state is peace.

## *wisdom spoke*

*"Too often am I left in scripture,
in scholarly texts and lectures.
Read but rarely lived.
Ever am I internalized
in the discursive thoughts of Man.
If you are reading this,
I need you to emancipate me
through your living deed."*

marya layth

*water ends and water begins*

In the end,
we are water running through
the fingertips of Life.

And in the end, there is no end.

For does water not turn into vapor?

## *hearsay*

I have heard talk of an apocalypse,
but I am no theologian—

> I cannot tell you if the end is near,
> or if the end is just the beginning.

I do not know if the skies will blacken,
but I do know that so many of our hearts
already have.

Apocalypse or not,
we must learn
that though knowledge is useful
and though money has its place
for the very bread we need to survive,
the only thing worth striving for is Love.

For beauty without Love is just vanity,
money without Love is just avarice,
and the eating of our daily bread without Love
is just gluttony.

When will we realize
that Humanity without Love
is simply savage?

# IV

The Star responded with its last words for The Girl,

"You seek me out for direction, yet you yourself are woven with stars."

The Girl looked at the The Star with doubt, but not disbelief.

As though to itself, The Star uttered with gravity and timbre:

"If only all knew of the galaxies within them, then none would settle to live for no more than bread."

And with that, The Star escaped her gaze.

The Girl effervesced in wonder, and vowed to herself that even if deafness were to steal her hearing, she would spend the rest of her days listening...

marya layth

...for that other voice.

*me too*

People do not need to be impressed;
they need to be inspired.

Few things are more inspiring to a soul
than saying:

Me too.

You struggle with the shadows?

Me too.

I know darkness,
I know it well.

But I also know of a light,
and it knows us well.

Let us walk towards it together.

*maps and soles*

The eternal list of maladies
that I once thought were remedies
could wrap around The Universe thrice.

Oh, how I chased the remedy
until my feet bled.

But now, when I look at my soles,
and the way the lacerations have healed,
and the way the scars have formed
from those jagged paths I once walked—

> I realize that there are two ways
> to interpret the abstract pattern
> of my wounds.

I could look at the pattern
and see only a meaningless mess
of scar tissue,
or I could read it
as the map
that it truly is.

One that I can forever reference
to help fellow navigators,
confused by those very roads,
learn to read the map of scars
on their soles too.

## *fellowship with gravity*

I am falling,
but I am also flying.

Oh, how easily do I descend—

for I find that when I do,
gravity is my dearest friend.

But as I take flight,
I find that every force of nature
works against me.

It is as if The Earth trembles
at the thought of losing me
and would rather see me fall
than have me discover I can fly.

And because I know this,
I can soar.

## *within grasp*

I cannot put an end
to all the cruelty around me.

I can, however, put an end
to all the cruelty within me.

## *heliotropism II*

For all of my struggles with pride,
I have always known
that I am not The Sun.

I am The Moon.

A vessel of light,
but not the light itself.

To be the sole bearer of light
is a burden I could not bare.

*high fate*

Chin up!

The Sky was made to be pondered,
and you mustn't keep her waiting.

## *from the sidelines*

If I could fight your battles, I would.

I would knock down each demon
that prowled within you
if only it were in my power to do so.

But we both know it is not.

It reminds me of the times
when I was the one taking the blows,
and they helplessly watched me fall
over and over again.

Yet they refused to keep score of my losses.

Their demons begged for stones,
but they knew throwing my failures at me
would only be another stumbling block
for these maladroit feet of mine.

And so, they let their demons starve.

Instead, they fed me the bread of their love,
the kind rarely doled out by human hands.

And now,
I will continue to fight.

Fight so you can fight.

Fight so I can tell you
that losing does not mean you are lost,

that you do not have to be perfect
to be loved,

and that you do not have to win every battle
to win The War.

*shoreline purpose*

I once reached for adventure
like the tides' relentless pursuit
to reach the shore.

But as it turns out,
there is a great journey right here,
in being where I am,
and much to be explored
while just looking at The Ocean.

## *reconciled*

Can it be that it was never about surviving,
that it was about living
*despite* the need
to survive?

## chasing the rise

We live in a world where we can succeed
—oh, we can succeed *wildly*—
without ever so much as touching a finger
on Virtue's hand.

And I think this is the defining moment
of our character:
our response
to the inevitable realization
that there is no need to be good
for goodness' sake.

Even so, I still say
that there is a need to work harder
than we have ever worked in our lives
to follow kindness wherever it goes.

Like the need to climb a tree
just for the sake of the view.

Or to chase the dark
just to be stilled by dawn.

## *somewhere along the way*

Though they will deride you
for striving towards
what is wise,
what is fair,
what is meek...

and though I do not know
why they do this,

I do know that when they say
giving makes you poor,
mercy makes you weak,
and purity is prude,
they are mistaken.

How many less hearts would I have hurt,
my own most of all,
had I not believed in their twisted truths?

And who are *they* anyway?
I do not know.

All I know is that there was a time
when I was small,
and my concept of Love was big.

But somewhere along the way
I began to harden myself,

*just like them.*

Still, a lot has happened along the way—

>   for upon it,
>   I have stumbled upon
>   a way.

It is a way so simple and so still
that even the movement of my lips
used to describe it
complicates the steady rhythm
in which this childlike heart
is being made within me...

*landscapes*

How absurd it would be
if The Sun were to dim its light
for The Stars.

If The Mountain were to shrink
for The Hills.

If The Ocean were to shallow
for The Streams.

And how much more absurd it is
when we dim, shrink, and shallow
simply because there are those
who wish we were less.

*races*

There is no need to run from death,
every step just steals our breath.

But do run.

Run to Life.

Run the race that has no need of lungs or legs.

The one that does not require
someone else to lose
in order for you to win.

The one that you can run while remaining
right where you are.

Ready. Set. Go.

Be still; Become.

*deaths and breaths*

They wanted to live lifetimes.

But a meadow once told me
you do not have to die and come back
in order to do that.

When the flowers within you wither,
let them.

Plant new seeds,
water them with the rainfall
of your sweat and tears,
and give them light by allowing the dawn
to rise on your night—

*no*
*matter*
*how*
*many*
*times*
*The*
*Sun*
*sets.*

And you will find that in this one lifetime,
you have experienced many deaths
and many first breaths.

*of what awaits*

There are still mountains in my heart
I have yet to climb.

## *sweet emancipation*

My soul
never felt
so free
as it did
when
surrendered.

## *for the meek: descent is illusory I*

One day I will sit beneath the flowers.

And one day I will be so patient
that I will actually see them grow.

And if I sit there long enough,
I will finally feel what it is like
to be crushed by the meekness
of a falling petal.

And I will open my heart just so
that it might find a home within me.

I just hope that I, too, can fall every good fall—

> like the fall of rain,
> ever descending
> towards its certain fate.

I pray to land on soil.

For my fall would be in vain
should I land on man-made roads—

> pavement has little need of rain.

No, I pray to be absorbed by The Earth herself,
who pulls me towards her thirsting lands
and calls me to be a part of it All.

I know you think I am just a drop—

    you are not wrong.

But even the smallest of small things
The Earth does not forget.

Unlike Man who too often neglects
the small things
because it reminds him that he, too, is small—

    he does not understand
    that there is something big,
    *something very big,*
    in being such.

## *for the meek: descent is illusory II*

And so I say,
I will fall the fall of rain.

And The Earth will open her heart
so I can live just beneath her chest
until The Sun, for whom I reach,
pulls me closer to her golden arms.

Because it was about The Sun all along.

Because it was never about the fall;
it was about the landing.

Landing in just the right spot.

Landing where I can bloom
towards the light beyond The Earth
where the wind cannot uproot me.

I hope one day they, too,
will sit beneath the flowers.

And that one day they, too,
will become so patient
as to see them grow.

And maybe they, too,
will sit there long enough
and finally feel what it is like to be crushed
by the meekness of a falling petal...

       ...perhaps even my own.

## the dialogue

"My sweet dear," they said to me,
"conscience never put bread on the table…"

"Oh, but it does!

"Just not at a table you choose to sit at.

"And with bread whose taste
you have yet to know."

If even you read nothing else but these last few sentences, know that I cherish the time you have given me. May light illumine your place on the path; the one we both walk, if even at different bends, and with different views. Wherever you are, know that my heart reaches and stumbles too...

But if you are one of the ones who traversed through every word of this book in order to get here, it means you have found the scattered seed. Or rather, that it has found you. I pray it grows into something beautiful, something fruitful, something that you can sit beneath to find shade.

Until next time, I bid you farewell. Thank you for being a part of my journey, and I hope I was a worthy part of yours.

Marya Layth

Marya Layth is driven by the desire to bring meaning to unfilled spaces, an obsession that leads her to the blank page time and time again. Marya finds refuge and strength in creativity, using it to express her unadulterated self—a self comprised of both chaos and love.

*More than Bread*, Layth's first address to the very world she commentates on, boldly and whimsically explores the duality of human nature through an illustrated tale of poetry and prose.

Marya Layth invites you
to sit beneath the night sky
with a girl who catches the attention
of a star.

Poems interweave
through the interaction between
the unlikely pair,
revealing the story of a heart that aches,
a heart that awes,
a heart that wonders why...

A heart like yours.

Made in the USA
San Bernardino, CA
02 October 2017